THE GREAT INDIAN CHIEFS

COCHISE • GERONIMO • CRAZY HORSE • SITTING BULL

ILLUSTRATIONS BY JEAN MARCELLIN
WRITTEN BY JEAN-ROBERT MASSON

BARRON'S

First edition for the United States
and Canada published 1994 by
Barron's Educational Series, Inc.

Copyright © 1994
by Editions Nathan, Paris.
First published as "Les Grands Chefs
Indiens" by Les Editions Nathan, Paris.

Translated from the French by:
Annie Heminway

All inquiries should be addressed to:
Barron's Educational Series, Inc.
250 Wireless Boulevard
Hauppauge, NY 11788

International Standard Book No.
0-8120-6468-2

Library of Congress Catalog Card No.
94-72397

Printed in France by Pollina,
85400 Luçon - n° 65771
4567   9886   987654321

FOREWORD

From the time the Spanish Conquistador Francisco Vasquez de Coronado swept across the Rio Grande in 1540 and entered North America, Native Americans discovered the brutal nature of the white man. Three centuries later, the same tragedy would be replayed with different actors.

Early in their history, ancient Native American civilizations were established in the Southwest territories. There, much later, the settled Pueblo watched the Apache hunters descend from the north, extending their range as far south as the Mexican desert. From 1860 on, when the pioneers threatened their territory, the Apache resisted, loyal to their leaders, Cochise and Geronimo. The first part of this book tells their story.

When the Spanish arrived, many diverse American Indian tribes occupied the land that stretched from Texas to the Canadian border, and from Mississippi to the Rocky Mountains. The Great Plains was a world in itself, where huge herds of buffalo, wild horses, nomadic peoples and big game hunters roamed. It was the ideal world for the Sioux. Masters of the bow and the lance, riders of mustangs almost from birth, the Sioux and their Plains allies fiercely resisted the invasion of settlers between 1860 and 1890, the greed of gold prospectors, and, later on, the arrival of the "blue coats"—the United States Cavalry. Their resistance was led by two men, Crazy Horse and Sitting Bull, told in the second part of this book.

The history of Native American peoples cannot be reduced to a few names alone, no matter how famous they are. Their stories, like the desert, seem to have no boundaries, and continue to grow.

CONTENTS

Sources and Suggested Readings

Arnold, Elliott, *La Flèche briseé*, Rocher, rééd, 1992.
Calloway, Colin G., *The First Americans*, Facts on File, 1991.
Carter, Forest, *Pleure, Geronimo*, Rocher, 1991.
Cole, Donald C., *Les Apaches Chiricahuas*, Éditions du Rocher, 1993.
Goble, Paul and Dorothy, *Custer's Last Battle, Red Hawk's Account*, Pantheon
   Books, 1969.
Griffith, A. Kinney, *Les Cent Premières Années de Nino Cochise*, "Points" Seuil,
   1989.
Grumet, Robert S., *Indians of North America*, Chelsea House, 1989.
Hassrick, Royal B., *Les Sioux*, Albin Michel, 1993.
Hyde, George E., *Histoire des Sioux*, Rocher, 1994.
MacDonald, Fiona, *Plains Indians*, Barron's Educational Series, Inc., 1993.
Mails, Thomas E., *L'homme-médecine des Sioux*, Rocher, 1992.
Rieupeyrout, Jean-Louis, *Histoire des Apaches et Histoire des Navajos*, Albin
   Michel, 1987, 1991.
Shorto, Russell, *Geronimo and the Struggle for Apache Freedom*, Silver Burdett
   Press, 1989.
Stan, Susan, *Native American People*, Rourke Publications, 1989.
Sweenay, Edwin R., *Cochise*, Rocher, 1993.
Thévenin, René, and Coze, Paul, *Mœurs et histoire des Indiens d'Amérique du
   Nord,* Petite Bibliothèque Payot, rééd, 1992.
Vestal, Stanley, *Sitting Bull*, Rocher, 1992.

Author's Note

I wish to express my debt to Jean-Louis Rieupeyrout. His seminal work, his exact-
ing research, and his passion left their imprint on a whole generation of people.

J.-R.M.

From the dawn of time, a People...

In the nineteenth century, the Apache occupied a vast area embracing northern Mexico, Arizona, New Mexico and southeastern Colorado. Historians date their arrival somewhere between 1000 to 1500 A.D. No one knows where they came from. An Apache legend talks about a migration of tribes that spanned forty generations. The Spaniards were the first Europeans to encounter them, in the sixteenth century. They called them *Apache,* which means

"enemies" in the Zuñi Indian language. Their territory was so big that it was divided into groups—in the east, the Kiowa hunted buffalo on the Plains; the Lipan and the Jicarilla, living among the Indians of the Rio Grande, grew corn. Further south lived the San Carlos and White Mountain tribes, the Mescalero and Chiricahua, all farmers and cattle breeders.

A tepee, a tent with a pole frame covered with buffalo skin—the dwelling of the Plains Indian hunters—corresponded to the *wikiup*, the Apache nomad hut made of branches and leaves.

The Apaches believed that human fate was determined by the clash of good and evil forces in the universe. To hold and use power well was to fulfill one's existence, even when confronting death. The community attached great importance to the initiation rites of the young, which prepared boys for their role as warriors.

As guardian of tradition, the chief handed down his power to his eldest son, with the consent of the tribal elders. "If another warrior proved clearly more courageous, intelligent or valiant, he was chosen instead. And unless a serious mistake had been made, nothing could change this decision." (Thévenin and Coze)

An Apache warrior. His face and entire body are ornamented with painted motifs with red as the dominant color, symbolic of violent action. The shaft of the spear is also painted and decorated with eagle feathers, and the leather-covered shield is painted with the totem of the tribe.

Native American civilization was based on a set of carefully regulated ceremonies. Songs and dances, like the Ghost Dance, the Buffalo Dance, and the Sun Dance, linked the tribes with the Supreme Being, the Great Spirit, the powers that rule the world, the gods worshipped by the tribe. For the Sioux and the Blackfoot, the Sun Dance involved tortuous initiation rites.

"The medicine man, also priest, sorcerer and healer, made four incisions in the candidate's chest, then inserted a small stick under the skin of each incision. The young man was then suspended by

10

thin leather thongs hanging from the top of a pole about 18 feet high. While fasting, he had to stare intensely at the sun. Swinging from the thongs, he blew into a whistle made of eagle bone, crying and singing challenges without stopping. Songs and drums accompanied his ordeal, which lasted until the sticks broke.

"At the end of the ceremony, the community sang songs of triumph for the young man as he emerged victorious from his trial. He showed his wounds with pride; now he was a warrior." (H. B. Alexander)

One of the episodes of the Sun Dance as it was practiced in the nineteenth century by many Plains tribes (Sioux, Blackfoot, etc.) and witnessed by travelers and ethnologists of that period. The dance took place in the middle of summer. The initiates first purified their bodies and minds under the supervision of a medicine man. Then, the ceremony opened with a dramatic act (shown here): The young men offered their blood to the Sun God—a tangible proof of the virtues of courage and determination they were supposed to have.

Cochise, Chief of the Chiricahua

Cochise was born around 1815 in southeastern Arizona at a time when his tribe, the Chiricahuas Chokonens, was at peace with the Mexican government. According to legend, he was the son of a Chokonen chief, descended from a long line of chiefs. His Apache name, She-Ka-She, which was probably given to him as an adult, was distorted by the Americans first into Chies, then Co-Chies, and later Cochise.

"To whom does the earth belong? I think it belongs to me. If you ask me for a part of it, I will not give it to you. I cannot give it up because I love it so much. All this land on each side of the river is mine....All this land is ours, and if you, my brother, ask me for it, I will not give it to you, for I love it, and I hope you will listen to me." (Chief Bear Rib, 1856)

The Butterfield Overland Company's stagecoaches, which connected Missouri to California via El Paso, Texas and Tucson, Arizona, traversed the heart of Apache territory. Some military forts protected this southern "Ox Bow Route," which the Indians for a long time refrained from attacking.

After Lieutenant Bascom's treachery, the Butterfield stagecoaches and their passengers were subjected to Cochise's attacks. These events inspired John Ford to make the famous film *Stagecoach*.

If, in 1861, Lieutenant George Bascom had not falsely accused Cochise of stealing cattle and kidnaping a young child, the fragile peace between the two communities would not have been broken. Instead, war between the Apaches and the Americans ravaged the Southwest for more than ten years.

Having escaped Bascom's trap, but with his men captured, Cochise intensified his raids against military patrols, travelers, and the stagecoaches that traveled via the Apache Pass, over 4500 feet high, venturing through the arid mountains near the border of Arizona and Mexico. One day, after attacking a relay station, Cochise captured two white men, whom he offered to exchange for Apache prisoners held by Bascom. The officer responded by hanging the Apache. The white hostages were then killed. After that, the Chiricahua chief no longer let up his attacks on the invaders. Arizona, New Mexico, and the Mexican province of Sonora resounded with the cries of raiding parties led by Cochise and Mangus Colorado. The whole Apache nation rebelled and for a short time appeared to be in control of its own destiny, from the Rio Grande in the east to the San Pedro river in the west.

At night, Cochise and his warriors left their hideaway in the Dragoon Mountains, which was later called "Cochise's Stronghold" or "Cochise's Fort."

"Cochise killed, pillaged, and burned." To defend himself, he attacked, unleashing a whirlwind of death throughout the Southwest. Everything was talked about: his cruelty and his bravery, his implacable hatred of the Americans and his thirst for peace, the fury of his raids and his efforts to ensure the Apache honorable conditions of survival." (Jean-Louis Rieupeyrout) Killing was to survive, to preserve the proud freedom of the desert... The whites were quick to denounce the means while forgetting the goal the Chiricahua chief sought.

"Because the reign of Cochise was marked by endless tragedies, by bloody raids against farmers, travelers and adventurers in his territory, myth began, associating him with an evil band of assassins. No Indian escaped this charge during that period. There was not a single white person who did not dream of killing a hundred Indians for every white man. On both sides, violence was uncontrolled. But did anyone think seriously about the cause of such fury? Did anyone try to stop the wave of hatred? Did anyone try to understand the Apache position?

"Cochise's revolt took place for similar reasons that, at the same time, drove Red Cloud and Crazy Horse to rise up against Carrington's soldiers. (See page 54.) Closer to home, Bascom's duplicity and deceitfulness made Cochise realize that treachery and lying were the fundamental elements of a policy whose goal was the destruction of all Native Americans. For men of honor like Mangus and Cochise, chiefs responsible for the fate of their people, what choice did they have other than violence?" (Simonin)

"The enemy fought without risking much, armed to the teeth, . . . well equipped to steal land and establish itself, hunt the Indians down, and remove them from the coveted world of the Plains. The crime was shared by both white man and red man; the actions lay between the 'extremes of civilization' and the 'extremes of savagery.' However, at the time an important distinction was not made: although the savagery existed on both sides, the motives of the Americans were not as honorable and legitimate as those of the Apache." (Simonin)

Golthlay, a young Chiricahua, whose courage in combat earned him the name Geronimo.

Chief Mangus Colorado at the head of a band of Mimbreno. "Although they were distinguished by their ability to carry out the most difficult and the most fearless deeds, the Mimbreno were not physically comparable to other Apache groups—the Mescalero, the Jicarilla, and the Chiricahua. Their cleverness and endurance made up for their lack of physical strength. No matter how cold or hungry an Apache may be, he never seems to be affected." (John Cremony)

The name of the elder chief of the Mimbreno Apache (a sub-group of the Chiricahua), who was the father-in-law, ally and friend in arms of Cochise, was Dasoda-Hae or Don-Ha, "He-who-is-seated-there." It is believed that he was born in 1792 and lived peacefully with his people near the banks of the Mimbres river in southwestern New Mexico. Brought up in a Hispanic-Mexican mission, he appeared one day dressed in a bright red shirt. He was given the name "La-Choy-Ko-Kunnoste," which means "Red Sleeves," or "Mangas Coloradas" in Spanish, and when Americanized became Mangus Colorado.

Quite early, Mangus decided to unite the Chiricahua against trespassing pioneers, miners, and surveyors. So he made an alliance with Cochise and the Chokonen, with the White Mountain in the West, and the Coyotero in the East. The federal government was concerned, and in 1852 offered a dishonorable treaty called Acoma, which was to leave the Mimbreno destitute. In 1859, a reversal took place: Mangus rejoined Cochise and Golthlay, a young Chiricahua from the Bedonkohe group. They made new raids on Sonora province in Mexico. According to one story, in the heat of battle, the young warrior's exceptional bravery so impressed the whites that they gave him a name that would become world famous—"Geronimo." Another version says that during the battle, the Sonorans were pleading with their patron saint, St. Jerome, for help, and that this is how Geronimo got this name. ("Geronimo" is Spanish for "Jerome.") (See page 28.)

In 1860, Mangus Colorado proposed a new alliance with Cochise, his brave cadet. The "Bascom incident" at Apache Pass was to ignite the flames of war.

"We were a great people living in these mountains. We lived well, in peace. One day, my best friend was captured by an officer of the white man and treacherously murdered. . . . The worst spot was Apache Pass. There, five Indians including my brother were killed and their bodies left to hang until they were reduced to skeletons. Now, Americans and Mexicans kill the Apache on sight. I have avenged them with all my might." (Declaration of Cochise to General O. Howard, 1873)

Apache Pass, place of repeated confrontations between Apaches and whites, was the site of a bloody ambush in July 1862. Seven hundred Chiricahua and Mimbreno took part, led by Cochise (left) and Mangus Colorado (right).

hen, in July 1862, a column of California Volunteers led by Colonel James Carleton headed east, following the route of Butterfield's stagecoaches, it had to cross Apache Pass. Given advance warning, Cochise and the Chiricahua and Mangus and the Mimbreno lay in ambush in the high rocks and opened fire on the soldiers, commanded by Captains Roberts and Cremony. The Americans returned fire with their artillery. The conflict lasted two days.

Mangus, wounded by a bullet, was taken to Janos, a nearby village, and treated by a Mexican doctor. There were deaths on both sides, without a victor. This bloody new episode led the army to build a fort on the site of the battle of Apache Pass, known afterwards as Fort Bowie. The fort enabled

travelers to move freely through the Chiricahua mountains. "The fort became an integral part of the landscape of southern Arizona, and was as violently hated by the Apache as it was by the soldiers who were forced to live there." (Edwin Sweenay)

Perhaps weakened by his wounds, and in spite of the hostility of those close to him, Mangus Colorado wanted to make peace with the "blue coats." Contacts were made and a trap was set. The old chief found himself in the hands of the California Volunteers. He was taken to Fort McLane, where General Joseph West insulted him. During the night, gunfire was heard. In the morning Mangus lay on the ground, dead, "killed in the attempt to escape," according to the official report.

From the range overlooking Apache Pass, Chiricahua and Mimbreno could observe the movements of enemy troops below.

Artillery fire, nevertheless, decimated Indian ranks. Cochise was
forced to withdraw, leaving nearby Apache Spring to his enemies.

Geronimo,
the Apache rebel

The end was approaching for Cochise. The brilliant defender of Apache freedom could do nothing to prevent the massacre of 800 Apache women, children and elders by Tucson settlers on April 30, 1871. Nor could he prevent the massacre of sixty Apache cut off by a Major Brown's troops in a Salt Canyon cavern. Then General Crook arrived, proposing a treaty to end the long years of suffering and mourning. The Chiricahua, Geronimo among them, refused for the most part and fled to Mexico.

Other groups agreed to settle on the San Carlos reservation in Arizona—a decision Cochise took. Tom Jeffries, a coachman of great integrity who became his blood brother, and General O. Howard, a trustworthy military man, convinced him to stop a dead-end war. Cochise died among his own people in the summer of 1874 on the Sulphur Springs reservation. A chapter of Native American history ended. For ten years, there was peace on Apache land. Then a new, somber wind arose with Geronimo.

The child was called Go-Hhla-Yeh, "He-who-yawns," or Golthlay, as the whites most often pronounced his name. He was born in 1823 or 1829, no one exactly knew, at Doyohn Canyon in eastern Arizona. His grandfather, Mahko, was chief of the Bedonkohe, a subgroup of the Chiricahua. He had eight brothers and sisters. He grew up like any other Apache child, dividing his time between domestic chores, play and initiation practice. As a novice (*diko-he*), he confronted "supernatural powers," the driving force of Apache society, which he had to learn to tame. When he was about fifteen, Golthlay participated in his first raid with older warriors. Armed with a bow and arrows, he was only allowed to round up cattle.

His new status was celebrated with a ceremony. A yellow vertical streak was painted on his face. He was sprinkled with sacred pollen, followed by songs and dances. Finally, he was given the trappings of a novice: a water-tube, a scratching stick, and a headdress made of eagle and hummingbird feathers. At the end of his initiation trial, the young man was admitted into the community of men and took part in tribal raids.

Unknown to the Indians before the arrival of the Spaniards, the horse of the Great Plains was a descendant of those abandoned by the Conquistadors in the New World long before. To catch a mustang with a lasso was a technique the Indians learned at a very young age.

In this scene, Golthlay is asking his future father-in-law for permission to marry Alope. The loom in the background is of Navajo origin.

At the age of seventeen, Golthlay was admitted into the Grand Council of warriors. Then he eloped with a young Apache woman called Alope, who belonged to the Nedni, one of the Chiricahua subgroups. Because marriage was the basis of Apache family life, Golthlay asked his future father-in-law's permission to marry Alope, for which he offered a dowry in kind. The ceremony took place according to tradition. The shaman (priest) married the couple, who had been separated, without seeing or speaking to each other for four days and nights. The tribe sang traditional songs celebrating "the sun, the beauty of the earth, and the

glory of the woman-painted-in-white, the divine priestess."

Later, this happy scene turned to tragedy. At the beginning of the summer of 1858, Mangus Colorado and the Mimbreno and Golthlay and the Bedonkohe rode towards Sonora to trade their craft goods for food. Near Janos in Mexico, they set up camp with their families. When they returned to the village some hours later, a desolate scene awaited them. Those left behind had been massacred by General Carasco's Mexican cavalry. Golthlay's mother and his three children lay on the ground, dead, near the body of his wife, Alope. The mournful group returned to Arizona.

Preceding the Americans, the Spaniards had initiated a policy of systematic destruction of Native American society. Distributed at will, especially to the Apache, bad alcohol destroyed their bodies and their spirits, enslaving those who thought they would find the white man's strength in it.

Galloping freely across Arizona's burnt land, Golthlay and Alope show their happiness before the slaughter of the summer of 1858.

"**S**everal days afterwards, we arrived at our village. There was nothing left, except the decorations that Alope had painted on the walls, and the playthings of our children. Then I burned everything, even our hut. I also burned my mother's lodge, and all that belonged to her. Because I could no longer find rest in what had been our peaceful home, why remain there? My father's grave was nearby, but when I visited it and recalled the happy days gone by, my heart suffered such sorrow that I left, swearing vengeance on the Mexican soldiers who had harmed me!" (Geronimo, some time later)

Golthlay and his tribe took one year to prepare their revenge. In 1859, with Mangus Colorado, Cochise and Golthlay heading the assault, they set out again for Sonora. The enemy, alerted, waited for them, but they were elusive.

They devastated the village of Alipse. The battle was so fierce, and Golthlay fought with such rage, that the Mexicans, terrified, gave him the name of their patron saint, Geronimo, a name by which he would always be known.

"The sun shone brightly as this spring afternoon ended. The *rancheria* was full of activity: women preparing supper, children running and yelling as they splashed in the small stream. It was a happy time.

Watching her children filled Alope with joy. She was completely satisfied. Golthlay loved his children as much as she did, without reservation. Life was good." (Forrest Carter)

In the spring of 1883, Geronimo's bands increased their raids on the southern territories.

June 1883. Geronimo's first surrender. General Crook forced the Chiricahua to lay down their arms.

Chief of the Chiricahua since the death of Cochise, Geronimo took refuge in the mountains of Mexico, launching raids throughout the Southwest. General Crook pursued him, scattering the Chiricahua into the Sierra Madre mountains, and forcing Geronimo to surrender.

For two years, Geronimo lived a quiet life as a farmer on the Apache San Carlos reservation in Arizona. But the call of freedom was strong. In 1885, with Nachez, the second son of Cochise, and a hundred dedicated warriors, Geronimo escaped.

Geronimo's flight. The Apache rebel escapes from the San Carlos reservation on the Gila river.

ree and surrounded by the Chiricahua, Geronimo again headed towards Mexico and the desert lands of the Sierra Madre, the place of so many confrontations between unforgiving enemies. General Crook sent his cavalry and infantry after him. Led by Captains Davis and Crawford, the "blue coats" encircled the camp, and the Chiricahua appeared to surrender. Geronimo asked to speak to Crook. "I wish to do what is right and nothing else," he told him. "I know that one has to die, but even if the sky should fall on my head, I want to do what is good. I have never done anything bad without cause. There is a god who sees us all; all of us are the children of this one god. He hears me. The sun, the night and the wind hear what we now say."

Then Geronimo agreed to surrender and took the northern trail towards Fort Bowie and exile. But the next day, tempting destiny, he decided to escape with a handful of followers to the Mexican Sierras. The illusion would be short-lived and the taste of regained freedom would be bitter. Determined to contain him at any cost, General Nelson A. Miles tracked down the Chiricahua chief. The adversaries met face to face at Skeleton Canyon. Miles promised to spare Geronimo's life, and had him sent to Fort Bowie on September 4, 1886.

With Nachez, Cochise's second son, at his side, Geronimo walks to meet General Nelson Miles in an Arizona canyon.

Over the years, the vastness of the Sierra Madre was the scene of confrontations between the Apache warriors, Mexican cattle breeders and merchants, American colonists and soldiers. Here a convoy of Mexican soldiers is encircled by Chiricahua cavalry.

A military wagon takes Geronimo and faithful Nachez to the "exile train" that took the Chiricahua prisoners to Florida.

What was to be done with the obstructive captive, Geronimo? The military chiefs did not consider the question long. On September 8, there was great excitement throughout Fort Bowie. The decision was made to take the Chiricahua to the nearby railway station.

"The members of the brass band of the Fourth Cavalry regiment were dressed in their parade uniforms. Two hours later, they lined up at the foot of the flagpole under the starred flag playing the *Star Spangled Banner*. A short distance away stood the wagons with the travelers' meager belongings. The garrison soldiers, also dressed in blue uniforms with white gloves, stood under the pavilion where Geronimo, Nachez and their families boarded the heavy vehicles. As the soldiers of the guard clicked their heels, the driver cracked his whip. The wagons moved out and headed towards the fort gate, escorted by a mounted detachment of soldiers led by Captain Henry Lawton. As they crossed the parade ground, the first strains were heard of the old nostalgic Irish ballad *Auld Lang Syne*, 'It's only a goodbye, my brothers.' General Miles was cynically amused. The convoy passed the guard house and descended the rough slope that led to the Northern trail. A halo of dust rose as it passed. Geronimo would never return." (Jean-Louis Rieupeyrout)

Washington D.C., March 4, 1905. Dressed in traditional deerskin leggings, his famous bandanna around his forehead, Geronimo marches past the new President of the United States, Theodore Roosevelt.

The Southern Pacific train was a frightening experience for the Apache. Who waited to slaughter them? The long journey towards the East ended in Florida. The men and women, separately, were confined at Fort Pickens and Fort Marion. More than 500 Chiricahua were to join them there. It was the end of the Apache saga.

The curtain rose on the last act—a side show. Brought to Alabama, the old chief was exhibited like some odd beast at state fairs in St. Louis and Omaha. He was photographed wearing a top hat, at the wheel of an automobile, the symbol of progress. He was converted to Christianity, and lived according to the white man's customs. On March 4, 1905, the President of the United States, Theodore Roosevelt, invited him to Washington for the inaugural parade. Marching in the gathering of notables were Geronimo, a Ute, two Sioux, a Blackfoot, and the Comanche chief, Quanah Parker. The crowd equally applauded the President and the "good savages."

Geronimo's exile, or the end of the Apache nation.

Geronimo died during a bout of pneumonia on February 17, 1909, on the Fort Sill reservation. He was buried with his whip, his saddle cover, and his turquoise jewelry.

Weep, O my people!

Crazy Horse and Sitting Bull,
two legendary Sioux in the eye of the storm

A Sioux village near Fort Laramie. Warriors, wives, old women, and children are busy tending their tepees.

In the vast territory that contains Kansas, Colorado, Wyoming, and the two Dakotas, a mosaic of tribes coexisted: Sioux, Crow, Mandan, Arapaho, Cheyenne, Arikara, Pawnee, Omaha, Ponca, Osage, Blackfoot, Gros Ventre, Assiniboine and more. But the central and northern Great Plains were the kingdom of the Sioux, the mustang, and the bison.

He was called Tashunke Witko, "Crazy Horse," in memory of an incident that occurred on the day he was born in 1842. As a young boy, he learned how to capture mustangs and draw a bow.

He was born around 1834 in the Sioux Hunkpapa group. His family were all warriors. He was first given the name of Slow, "He who thinks slowly." At the age of ten, he rode a pony. A little later, he wounded his first enemy, a Crow Indian, and killed his first bison. It was then that his father gave him the name Sitting Bull.

Lord of the Great Plains, the buffalo was, for the Sioux, a god sometimes identified with the sun. Sacred dances invoked its name. Protector of men and women, it was revered by hunters. "Its meat was the basis of their diet. Its skin provided them with clothes, bedding and tepees, and went into the making of canoes and the hunting-harnesses of horses. From the bones, the Sioux sculpted all kinds of instruments. From its hooves, they made glue, and from its tendons, cords for bows. Its blood was used for paint, its horns for spoons, bowls, adornments, and weapons. Bison dung provided fuel for fire. The lives of Sitting Bull and his people depended on the bison. Without it, they were lost." (Stanley Vestal)

The legend tells that one night, the young Crazy Horse had a premonition: he was going to be a chief of his people. "The Indian is mystic to a degree that one finds nowhere else except among oriental ascetics or Christians: I do not believe that there is another people in the world that is as dedicated to visions. Both men and women can seek this mystic communion between themselves and the spiritual powers of the world. The seeker withdraws alone, fasts and waits for the revelation that, perhaps will bring the powers to him." (H. B. Alexander). The visions described by Native-American prophets at the end of the last century were the origin of the Ghost Dance.

"In early spring, we traveled to the high plateaus near the Rocky Mountains where the greatest herd of wild horses in the world lived. We had been following a fresh track for five days when we encountered our first herd. We noticed a large, iron gray stallion. Our guides told us that this superb horse was the leader of the herd. He began to prance, lifting his head as high as his proud stature permitted, and threw lightning glances at us from his blazing eyes. Then we saw him, his head erect against the sky, sounding a cry of distress and defiance. Never had he known such humiliation: his herd, which always followed his slightest order, now savagely trampled him. Finally, he disappeared . . .

"This horse acquired the reputation of a night rover throughout the Northwest. One often saw this creature of the night, silent and alone, stopping at the top of a butte. In the moonlight, his silhouette looked like a statue. Because of his habits and because his tail and mane sometimes appeared almost phosphorescent, he was called Shunka-tonka-Wakan, 'Ghost Horse.'" (Tale of Chief Buffalo Child Long Lance)

Native Americans practiced ritual painting on their skin with a mixture of fat and colored substances. "Each color was symbolic. Red evoked violent feelings, the devastating fires of combat as well as the fire of love. Blue was the color of peace and happiness. White was the color of youth and innocence. It was also sometimes a sign of mourning, as black was often a sign of misfortune. These shades, especially green and yellow, could be interpreted variously, according to their arrangement or the form of the signs for which they were used." (Thévenin and Coze)

A warrior people, the Sioux scalped their dead enemies. "The scalp dance, was done at night by torchlight. It was repeated fifteen nights in a row, the warriors brandishing their weapons and bragging about their exploits to a group of women who waved the new scalps on sticks and stamped their feet on the ground. The dancing was truly frenetic. The warriors yelled fearsomely, and threatened each other with their weapons with such violence that it seemed they were going to kill each other. Their terrifying act, under torchlight, was something fantastic. When the dance was over, the trophies were buried with songs of mourning, full of pain and pity." (George Catlin)

The Sioux, who did not understand their neighbors, the Cheyenne, very well, called them the "People-with-the-foreign-language" or the "Red Speakers." Their common past brought them together. In the middle of the last century, the Sioux and the Cheyenne had to leave the rich territory of Minnesota near the Canadian border, chased away by the white settlers' greed and betrayed by government treaties that no one respected.

The exiles moved to the southeast of what is today Colorado. They found arid land there, without vegetation or game, crossed by thin, sandy rivers like Sand Creek. And there again, they encountered the aggressive hostility of white settlers.

They were threatened by famine. Joining their forces, the Arapaho, Sioux, Cheyenne and Kiowa attacked Butterfield's stagecoaches, pillaged, burned farms, and killed. However, Chief Black Kettle of the Southern Cheyenne wanted to live in peace. At the request of Governor Evans, he agreed to regroup his tribe near Fort Lyon. This situation was intolerable for the "Volunteer Legion of Colorado," grouped in Denver under the command of Colonel J. M. Chivington. They set out for Fort Lyon to get artillery reinforcements. Six hundred men advanced at night along the Sand Creek river, until they reached the edge of Black Kettle's Cheyenne camp.

The Legion of Colorado Volunteers encircle the Black Kettle Cheyenne. Despite the white flag, they were slaughtered pitilessly.

The Cheyenne camp set up on a bend in the Sand Creek river. Men, women and children with their tepees: the opening at the top released smoke and allowed light to enter. A draught horse; dogs, whose flesh was a delicacy; skin drying: the last moments of a peaceful life.

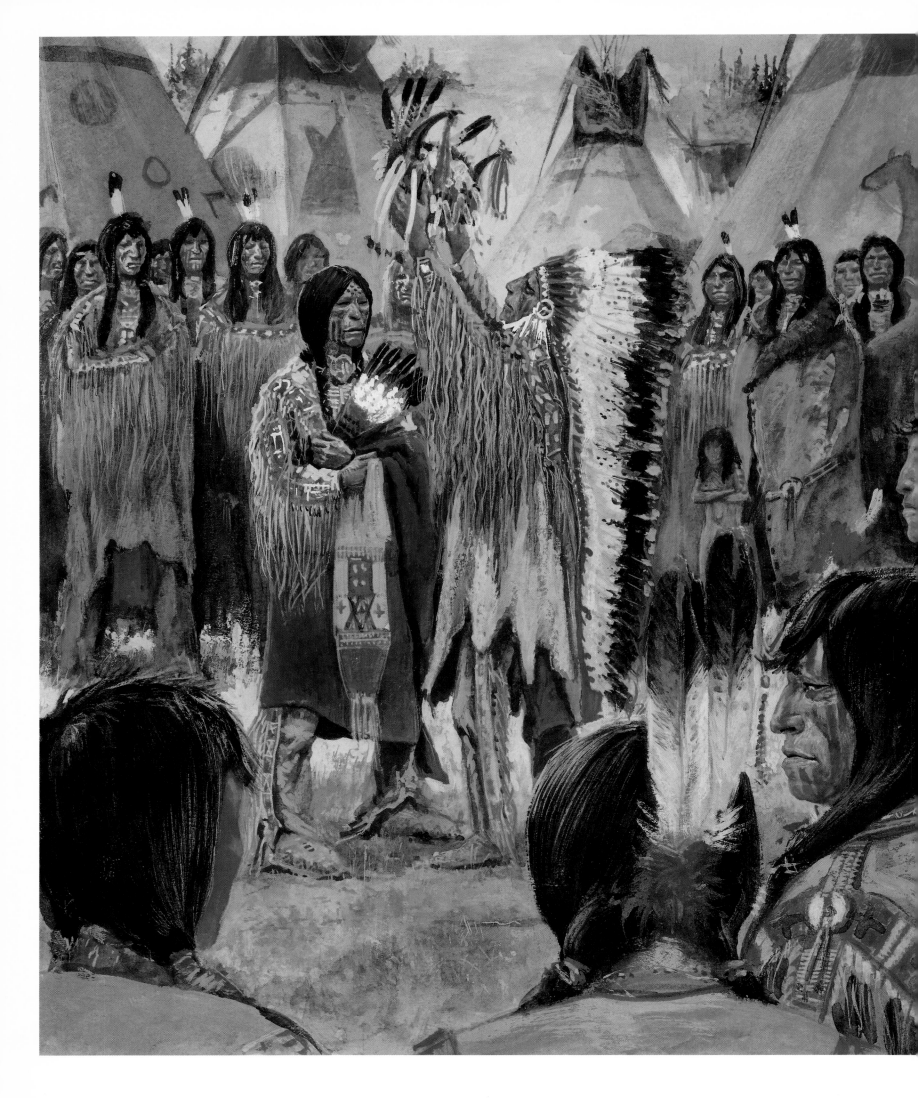

The Cheyenne who survived the massacre of Sand Creek took revenge by burning farms in northern Colorado.

"On November 29, 1864, at dawn, the Colorado Volunteers advanced on foot from the south with their sharpshooters spread out. They began shooting at once, marching on the village, where those who woke up first rushed outside the huts. There were white soldiers everywhere. Horses crashed against the tepees. Men rushed out of their shelters, half naked. Black Kettle hoisted the American flag on a flagpole in front of his tent, in the middle of the village. Under that, he hung a white flag. Gunfire. Some Indians fell. Some managed to reach their ponies and flee. Black Kettle was now in the center of a group that had swarmed around him. The soldiers, he thinks, will not fire on men, women and children taking refuge under the American flag. They fire, however, at everyone and everything they see. Chief White Antelope stands before his hut, a bison robe draped around him and arms crossed, singing his death song. Black Kettle understands that the massacre will be total. His wife falls at his side. Some women advance towards the soldiers. They fall, killed at point blank range. Within the circle of tents is a carousel of death. Children cry. Black Kettle flees after trying to rally his overwhelmed warriors around him. Chivington had said, 'Kill them all, old and young.' " (Jean-Louis Rieupeyrout)

Chivington's tally was more than 150 dead, more than 100 scalps, three children captured. In a theater in Denver, he exhibited the "trophies" at each performance. But Black Kettle was still around and the survivors were filled with a raging desire for revenge.

1865. The Sioux, for their part, contented themselves to see the whites moving away. The Civil War had ended, freeing entire regiments of "blue coats" for other tasks. Crazy Horse and Sitting Bull (shown left, as he is being made chief by the Grand Council of the Sioux Hunkpapa) will soon return to the forefront.

Expert at taking advantage of every crevasse of the terrain, at home on the plains as well as in the mountains, the Sioux and Cheyenne used a coded communication system to watch the road and warn their camps of the approach of the enemy with smoke signals.

In Wyoming and Montana the Bozeman Trail, blazed by John Bozeman—starting at Fort Laramie and continuing by the Big Horn Mountains—gave miners and gold seekers access to mineral rich Virginia City, in northern Montana. Soldiers kept watch on the trail that crossed Sioux territory. Perhaps the great Sioux chief, Red Cloud, would have left the trail open to miners if Colonel Carrington, at the head of 600 men, had not used it to stake out his forts. Red Cloud convinced Crazy Horse of a plan: besiege Carrington in Fort Kearny, then unite a coalition of 3000 warriors—Sioux, Oglala, Hunkpapa, Brulé, Cheyenne. The Indians ambushed and killed eighty soldiers and their commander, William Fetterman. After bloody reactions from the other side, the army understood the necessity of negotiating a settlement. Red Cloud insisted that the forts along the trail be evacuated. The last soldier had barely left when the Sioux and Cheyenne set the Fort Kearny barracks ablaze.

The guns recovered by the tribes did not equal the firepower of the carbines that American troops carried. The new repeating Springfield ravaged the ranks of the Sioux and forced Red Cloud to withdraw from the battle of Wagon Box in 1867. Ten years later, the famous Winchester 73 with fifteen rounds appeared.

The Cheyenne had set up camp on the Washita river in Colorado. Hunting had been good, and winter would be mild. But almost four years to the day after the Sand Creek massacre in November 1864, a troop of 700 men, under the command of twenty-nine-year-old officer George Custer, circled their tents and fired without warning, shooting men, women, and children, and killing their chief, Black Kettle. From that day on, Custer would be known by all the Indians as "the Squaw Killer."

In 1868, after the Sioux victory over Carrington (see page 54), Red Cloud, Crazy Horse and Sitting Bull (right) considered themselves masters of an immense area of the Great Plains, from Missouri to the Rocky Mountains.

The day after the massacre at Sand Creek, General Hancock's troops attempted to reestablish order on the Kansas plains, where bands of Arapaho, Cheyenne, and Kiowa continued to rebel. Their expedition having failed, the government thought the moment had come to propose a peace treaty to the Indians that would at least recognize their right to live. A peace commission was given the responsibility of carrying the good news to the tribes. It was greeted with skepticism, if not hostility, by the chiefs. The Crow, chief Beartooth, told Commissioner Taylor: "Call back your young men from the Big Horn Mountains. They burned our land. They killed our animals—elk, deer, antelope, bison—not to eat but to let rot. If I went into your territory to kill your cattle, what would you say?"

The situation remained unresolved. Once again violence followed. On November 27, 1868, on the Wichita River, the Seventh Cavalry Regiment, headed by a young ambitious officer, Lieutenant-Colonel George Custer, repeated the massacre at Sand Creek blow for blow. (See page 53.) More than 100 Cheyenne lost their lives. Their chief Black Kettle was killed, and the survivors were deported to a reservation. Thus the first great period of Indian wars ended in the central and northern parts of the American continent.

ight years later, in 1876, the Montana territory bordering the Canadian frontier, would become the setting of a new and final clash between the federal forces and the Sioux tribes.

The rush of prospectors toward the Black Hills across Sioux country in search of gold, the proposition of the government to buy the "Black Hills," an area sacred to the Sioux (rejected by Sitting Bull and Crazy Horse with contempt), the presence of Custer, "the killer of squaws," in Montana—so many firebrands threatened to ignite the fires of war.

In February 1876, General Terry's raid—supported by Custer—launched against Crazy Horse was merely a prelude to a more important confrontation.

Aware of imminent danger, Sitting Bull sought to assemble the forces of the Indian nations. He held a Grand Council at Chalk Buttes, on the Tongue river. Crazy Horse was present. The Cheyenne of the North and the Arapaho joined them. Tepees flowered over the plain near Rosebud. An impressive Indian coalition gathered around the most respected chiefs: Sitting Bull, Crazy Horse, Red Cloud, Two Moons, He-Dog, Black Moon, Gall, Spotted Eagle, Fast Bull, Old Bear, Big Road. The hour of destiny had arrived.

Preparing for war. Whites and
Indians assemble their forces,
each spying on the other's camp.

Lieutenant-Colonel
George Armstrong Custer.

"—Crook's column of six hundred men will leave
from Fort Fetterman and march toward the north,
crossing the Powder, then the Tongue River. His mission will consist of pushing the Sioux in the direction
of the Yellowstone River towards which:

—Gibbon's column of four hundred and thirty
men will march from Fort Ellis (Montana). They will
join with:

—Terry and Custer's column of eight hundred
men coming from Fort Lincoln (Dakota).

These three columns will drive the Sioux before
them, forcing them into a trap south of Yellowstone."

(The American Offensive Against the Sioux,
General Terry's Plan)

Cheyenne scouts watch as General Crook's column approaches Rosebud, where Indian tribes have gathered.

At the end of May, the columns began their march as planned. Colonel Terry left Fort Lincoln accompanied by Custer's Seventh Cavalry. General Gibbon had already left Fort Ellis. As for General Crook, he left Fort Fetterman, stringing out his cavalry, his infantry, wagons and 600 mules. On June 16, Crook reached the banks of the Rosebud. One thousand white soldiers and Indian scouts, Crow and Snake, rallied, almost touching their enemies. Indeed, hundreds of tepees of the gathered tribes were set up nearby on a tributary of the Little Big Horn.

Imagine a more perfect contrast. Throughout the second weekend of June, the Sioux, camped on the Rosebud, celebrated the Sun Dance. (See pages 10 and 11.) The chief of the dancers, Sitting Bull, had a premonitory vision: the soldiers would come and fall in his camp, sign of a great victory to come.

At that moment, the Cheyenne spotted Crook's column and alerted Sitting Bull. A thousand Sioux and Cheyenne moved towards the soldiers, hiding behind a hill overhanging the Rosebud river. The Crow scouts rushed back to Crook's camp screaming "Lakotas! Lakotas! Sioux! Sioux!"

The battle began on June 17 at dawn. The fighting was intense. The Sioux and Cheyenne, who had neither a joint military strategy nor a unified command, attacked the soldiers in small groups, free to act on their own initiative. Sitting Bull encouraged his brothers, but weakened by the physical torture of the Sun Dance, did not fight himself. "Throughout the fighting, the Indians showed astonishing fierceness. The old tactic of remaining at a distance and circling the enemy, thus taking minimum risks, was no longer relevant. A new spirit motivated the warriors, who charged at a gallop on their ponies, plunging like devils into the midst of the soldiers, often confronting them in terrible hand-to-hand combat." (George Hyde) There was neither conqueror nor conquered. The Americans and Indians withdrew to their positions.

The battle on the Rosebud. Hand to hand combat between Sioux and Cheyenne against Crook's infantry and cavalry.

"Indian attacks take place at daybreak or evening, never at night, so that each warrior's 'exploits' can be checked. They are always preceded by a war cry, a sharp piercing note that resounds for a long time." (Thévenin and Coze)

The battle of Little Big Horn, the hill where George Armstrong Custer met his death. White Bull, Sitting Bull's nephew, stated afterwards that he delivered the fatal blow to Custer.

The military leaders consulted each other. Colonel Terry ordered Custer to head for the junction of Big Horn and the Little Big Horn tributary, where he would be joined by Gibbon's column to trap the Indians in a vice. Terry had seen correctly. The Indian village had strung its tepees on the same banks of the Little Big Horn. Lieutenant Bradley noted in his journal: "This will be one of the greatest battles against the Indians ever fought on this continent. A united force like ours is invincible."

Glory drove Custer more than anything else, and he was ready to do anything to make it his. He reached Little Big Horn on June 24. The next day, he divided his men into three detachments: Reno's, Benteen's and his own. Then, ignoring Crook's instructions and without waiting for Gibbon, he charged.

The battle raged for two days. Sitting Bull, Crazy Horse, Gall, Black Moon and hundreds of warriors first met Reno's detachment. The "blue coats" fell "like bison during a hunting party." Then Custer arrived, moving along the Little Big Horn, certain of victory. The Sioux chased after him. A massacre followed. "When Custer reached the hill where he was killed, he was probably aware that his detachment was doomed. Half his officers and men had already perished. The others had been divided into small groups and each of them was being assailed by a horde of warriors on horse and foot hurling themselves into the fighting with passion, determined not to give in." (George Hyde)

The total count? On the American side, 277 soldiers were killed. The Indians lost only twenty-
six warriors.

On June 26, around noon, as the Sioux found out
that fresh troops were moving up the Little Big
Horn—Terry's and Gibbon's cavalry—they spared
the lives of Reno and Benteen, and returned to their
tents. Then, after setting fire to the prairies around
them, they withdrew to the Big Horn mountains, taking with them the considerable booty they had captured on the battlefield.

Custer's defeat and death was felt as a tragedy by
the American people. A Civil War hero, "General"
Custer, defeated by the Indians! Criticism, however,
was endless. His foolish pride was condemned, his
lack of discipline, his obsessive taste for honors, his
racist contempt and misunderstanding of his oppo-
nents, the lack of preparation of his troops, and the
poor quality of his command. The army, though,
dreamed of revenge.

Sitting Bull learns that Custer and
all his men perished. According
to one version, where the facts
contradict the legend, Custer was
not scalped, not because the
Indians held him in any particular
awe, but because he had cut his
long hair just before the battle.
His corpse was stripped but not
mutilated by the Sioux women,
perhaps as part of their tradition.

The twilight of a People

Crazy Horse's body was placed, according to Sioux ritual, on a funeral scaffold. His family kept watch for three days and three nights.

The Indian victory changed nothing in the course of things. During the summer of 1876, the encounters started again in the Plains. General Nelson Miles (who had received Geronimo's surrender) attacked Chief Dull Knife's Cheyenne. Crazy Horse himself had to withdraw from the American carbines. Would he abandon the struggle as his brothers-in-arms, Sitting Bull and Red Cloud, would end up doing? He refused. He was a warrior and would remain one. He headed towards the Big Horn mountains. But his time had run out. On May 6, his kin having persuaded him, he went to Fort Robinson in Nebraska, surrounded by 1100 survivors of his people—men, women and children. He was treated like a common prisoner. When he resisted imprisonment, a soldier bayoneted him in the back. In this way Crazy Horse, the boldest of the Sioux chiefs, died.

The army regained control of the Plains. The Sioux, hunted and deprived of their sacred animal, the bison, lived after that as outlaws. Sitting Bull concluded that only one country on the vast continent could offer his people refuge—Canada, the country of The-Mother-Of-All (Queen Victoria).

The journey to the north was a long march with unexpected detours. Sitting Bull's Sioux first left for the southeast in the area near the Yellowstone River, then headed east. During the winter of 1876, they were attacked by a detachment of Americans and lost some horses. Sitting Bull then headed towards the Sioux sanctuary of the Big Horn mountains. But Crazy Horse was no longer there. The fugitives were tormented by hunger. They had not found a living animal on their route. They finally arrived in "red coat" country. This was a small happy interlude at the end of their wanderings.

Canada grew impatient. Why did the United States not take back the Sioux? A commission visited Sitting Bull in October 1878 at Fort Walsh, proposing peace and a "pardon." Sitting Bull refused. However, the situation continued to deteriorate. The Indians were short of food. On July 10, 1881, Sitting Bull crossed the frontier followed by 187 Sioux, and on July 19, at Fort Buford, he surrendered his arms and horses in exchange for a "pardon" granted for his past actions. "He was nothing but an old Indian," observed William Bowen, a young officer. "We have before us a broken man."

Sitting Bull and his Sioux warriors during their long march towards the Canadian border.

Sitting Bull became a circus attraction, as Geronimo would several years later—the major attraction of the Wild West show of "Colonel" William Frederick Cody, alias Buffalo Bill, at the end of nineteenth century America.

Sitting Bull and Buffalo Bill in London, before Queen Victoria.

Am I wrong to love my own law?
Is it bad for me to have red skin?
Because I am a Sioux?
Because I was born where my
father lived?
Because I am ready to die for my
people and my country?

(Sitting Bull)

During this time, on the Sioux reservation in Dakota, a mad hope arose for the arrival of a new age, marked by the disappearance of the white man, the return of the buffalo, and the resurgence of Indian power.

The Ghost Dance was the catalyst of this great hope. It was rumored that Sitting Bull was the head of this spiritual resistance movement, that he was the New Messiah. The authorities were alarmed. On December 15, 1890, on the order of whites, Indian police came to arrest him. There was confusion. Gunshots. Sitting Bull was dead.

78

Oh, Sun! You are eternal!
But us, Kaitsé'nko, we die!
Oh Earth! You last forever!
But we, Kaitsé'nko, we die.

(Death song of the Omaha Sioux)

What is life?
It is a firefly shining in the night.
It is the breath of a buffalo in winter.
It is the small shadow that runs in the grass.
and vanishes at sunset.

(Crowfoot, Chief of the Blackfoot)